WHERE DID YOU GO,
MR. KITSEL?

A BOOK OF POEMS

WHERE DID YOU GO, MR. KITSEL?

❧

Daniel A. Heller

DCDESIGN BOOKS | *Brattleboro, Vermont*

Printed in the United States

10 9 8 7 6 5 4 3 2 1

At DCDESIGN BOOKS, publisher/designer Dede Cummings has
created a publishing imprint that acquires books that tell literary
and compelling stories with a focus on writing about place.

DCDESIGN BOOKS
34 MILLER ROAD
WEST BRATTLEBORO, VT 05301
www.dedecummingsdesigns.com

ISBN: 978-1-950584-20-8

DANIEL A. HELLER'S WEBSITE:
www.educationalcapabilities.com

COVER ART:
Donald Saaf
http://donaldsaaf.com

As always, forever, and once again,
For Nina.

❧

CONTENTS

❦

WHERE DID YOU GO, MR. KITSEL?

A BOOK OF POEMS

A WORLD WITHOUT HOPE

Bow before the Lord Kindness,
Who builds the conduits
Between hearts,
Who connects us to all else,
And makes existence possible.
Defeating anger, envy, and hate,
Kindness
Trumps all conflict
And dismissal.
No need to keep
One's guard up.
No need to fear oppression.
A central teaching,
The core of education.
What good is math
In an atmosphere of
Fear?
How will we support each other
Without it?
The failure to teach
Kindness
Is like teaching how to
Build a fire
But not how to
Put it out.
A world of kindness
Does not even
Need hope

ANGER

I sense another fight is near.
The switch for anger in my head
Has flipped and loosed the choking snake
Which coils around my self-control.

It makes my chest constrict, my breath
A chore, my heart compressed so tight
Its beating floods my ears and mind.
I must give in, no choice remains.

The anger forces words and acts
That have no business to exist,
And yet they are and hurt my love.
They make her cry and make me wince.

As time goes by I can't recall
What caused the fight, the switch
To flip. I only know that I
Am filled with sadness, myself to blame.

Whoever said those words and did
Those awful things could not be me
But someone else who took control
Of my sad self; that's all I know.

I want to tell her "Sorry for my
Harsh words," my unacceptable
Violations of her sweet self.
But I am frozen, cannot act.

Even though the anger's leaving me,
I'm prisoner still; a greater force

Than I controls what I can do,
And so I stand a foolish man.

I cannot give the hug she needs,
Nor give the kiss required now.
I'm frozen in my guilt and shame,
And vicious anger at myself.

The only cure to wait the slow
Abatement of the falling fire
And hope that once again she can
Forgive my horrid inner rage.

April Snow

A temporary nuisance,
Leaving behind
Slippery slush and mud,
Dashing hopes of
Summer warmth and sunshine.
Nature doesn't ask
Permission or
Forgiveness.
It just is,
And we have the illusion
Of control
At best.
All we can do
Is to
Accept gracefully
What is not ours
To alter.

BIRD'S NEST

I

For years I'd been
Self-cleansing.
Painfully twisting
Like a dishcloth
To wring out
The old
Anger and pain,
Regret and paranoia,
Aggression and violence.
Then bathing in
The warm waters
Of compassion and kindness,
Soaking up all I could.

II

And then,
There was
The bird's nest,
Just above and to the right
Of my front door.
A sign.
My new self,
Acceptable to the world.
The spirit of Nature
Chose me,
Or should I say anointed me,
To provide a safe haven
For this small creature.

First eggs,
Then chicks.
The mystery of life
Had been presented
For me to witness.

III

But when I'd leave
Through the door—
Fluffing and fluttering,
Chaotic, panicked flights,
Darting aggressively.
Did I cause this?
Was I so threatening,
So fear inspiring?
What did this
Little bird think of me?
Ah, *think of me*.
Animals do not think.
They know.

Blur

Over forty years together.
The lines blur.
What is I? What is you? What is we?
You have become elemental to my life,
Like sunshine, rain, and laughter.
I lived at one time without you.
I no longer remember how.
If you were to leave,
I would wake to a frightening
And foreign world.
Unrecognizable.
I would stumble along,
Searching for a path,
Finding none.

BULLET

In choosing my
Means of travel,
I chose the Bullet Train,
And that has defined
Everything since.

Outside the windows
A beautiful blur,
All the world in
One indistinguishable
Flowing riot
Of rushing canvas.

I remain motionless
Except for the gently swaying,
Rushing from destination
To destination,
Never arriving.

CARE

Piston legs,
Bellows breath,
The bike going nowhere.
The instructor
Calls out orders
For cadence and resistance,
But adds,
"Always take care of
Yourself."

The snake with the yellow head
Falls from above.
There is a little boy on the seat.
Put on your own mask
First.

After the storm,
You cannot help others
Before you extricate
Yourself
From the rubble.

CARPE DIEM

A tiny kiss,
A mere peck
No bigger than a mustard seed,
Can contain the fierce love
Of a mother,
The tender love
Of a partner,
The comfortable love
Of a friend.
Such a small gesture;
No trouble at all,
To say so much.
I forgot to kiss you today,
But no matter,
There will
Always
Be tomorrow.

CHAOS AND CRUELTY

The soft buzzing of bees
Reciting their humming mantra
Meditatively searching from blossom to blossom.
Oblivious to the world,
Oblivious to themselves,
Obsessed with their work.
Sunrise to sunset.

Tirelessly occupied
With their sacred mission
Not even known to themselves:
To produce sweetness and life
In the midst of chaos and cruelty.

COMPLETE

Hold my hand
And let your life flow through mine.
I have ceased to be one individual person,
And I need you to be complete.
I see with both of our eyes,
Smell with both of our noses,
Touch with both of our hands,
Taste with both of our tongues,
Hear with both of our ears.

The world has no meaning to me,
But only to us.
We have lived as one so long
That I have forgotten
How to be one person.
Everything is defined
To me through you.
I am scared to be alone.

Together we are one person
While being two halves.
A half may be able
To function,
But not completely,
And what completes me
Is you.

CONVENIENCE

Death is never convenient.
There is the garden project to begin.
There is too much homework.
We were going to take a trip.
No one sent notice,
Or checked calendars,
Or checked dates and availability.
What are we supposed to do?
Drop everything?
Is there a choice?
The living need our comfort
And support.
So we go,
Forgetting what was to be done,
And offer ourselves
And love.

CRACKS

I had a second glimpse of the end.
As if I need convincing
Of impermanence.
The walls of time
Are closing in.
Cracks, fissures, fault lines—
Subtle but sure.
The only absolute now
Is to live
As I should have lived
All my life,
With the knowledge
Of imminent dissolution.
How many more
Gardens will I plant?
How many more time times
Will I say
I love you?

CROCUS

There you are,
Cute little crocus
With your snow cap
At a fetching angle,
Once again
Bringing the lie:
Rebirth and renewal,
Rejuvenation and revival.
I feel myself
Getting sucked in,
But my trembling hands
And weak eyesight
Tip me off.

Dad

Stupid old man,
He thought.
What an idiot.

Who could be so foolish
To get in the shower
Wearing a money belt?

And then there was the panic
And the shame.
What was there to do?
Would the money be destroyed?

He had to tell her.

There was no snicker,
Rolling eyes,
Sigh,
Reprimand.

Only quiet understanding
And loving confidence.

She simply took the bills,
Laid them out on the bed,
And left to get her hairdryer.

DAFFODIL

What if
When you die
There are no daffodils?

How will I show you
That I remember and cherish
Our first moments
Of connection?

How will I show you
That I honor that girl,
So playful and kind,
Gentle and loving?

If
When you die
There are no daffodils,
I will turn myself into
A daffodil
And lay myself by your side.

I will honor you,
Celebrate you,
Remember you

And that our first flower
Was a daffodil.

DARKNESS

Today is dark.
The clouds cover the sun
Like the curtains
At the end of an act.
Not the last act.
There will be more
At some future time
I cannot imagine now.
Today the darkness dampens
My heart with a dull ache
And a claustrophobia
That sucks up all the air.
I love you.
Love brings joy.
Love brings sadness.
For now,
I can only
Dedicate myself to you
And wait.

DIRGE

"Where are the songs of spring?"
They were for other ears,
Not those I wear now.

Replaced with a dirge for youth,
Inspiring a young man's yearning
In an old man's body.

The cruel seductions of spring
Bring unreachable goals
And unfullfilable desires.

I must rest now,
Not listen to this music,
But sing my own song.

Dots

We are always saying
Goodbye,
Turning smaller and smaller
Until we are dots
And then nothing.

EXISTENCE

I cannot outlive you.
Without you there is no life,
Just a solid, silent existence
Slowly revolving from day to day
By habit.
The headless pillow,
No warm belly
Pressed against my back,
No playful poking.
The sun will shine.
The birds will sing.
The mice will multiply.
They don't care
Or know,
Or care to know.
Time will pass,
And I will wait darkly
For what comes next.

Faith

I see endless fields of stars,
Flowers blooming,
Single cells becoming human beings.

I understand nothing.

I have two choices:
Believe it all means something,
(Despite my ignorance),
Or accept the random meaninglessness
Of everything.

One path takes faith.
The other leads to despair.
I choose faith.
What else can I do?

What about me, then?
With all my flaws
And faults,
With all my strengths
And efforts to be good.

Can I be,
Could I have been
Anything other than what I am
And have been?

Could I have been someone else
And still be me?
I am who and what
I am

Without blame or praise.
But I don't
Know why.

The lingering questions—
Have I been
Good enough?
Am I an acceptable
Human being?
Could I have
Changed my life's course
In any way?

Do I have meaning?

FATHERS AND SONS

We grow up;
We grow older.
Selves and relationships
Evolving—
Tendrils of smoke
In the air.
A father nurtures his son,
Holding, advising, protecting.
Giving total support
And never letting go.
Sons leave
Without separation.
Fathers and sons
Grow apart and
Meld,
Like two tree trunks
That grow into each other,
Sharing their essences.
Each becomes the other.
One life while living
Separately.
A double helix.
Each holding up the other.
Roles merge and shift
As the son becomes the supporter
And the father the supported.
Still the man supports the boy
Even while being supported by him.
Always there to help
While being helped.
The bond breaks only with death.
Then the son,

Now a father,
Continues the cycle
With his own boy.
Eternity in mortality.

FIREFLIES

Do you remember,
We'd all go out on the deck
On July nights
To watch the fireflies?
You would shout out
Bizarre phrases
(Something about frolicking naked)
Because you said that loud noises
Made them more active,
Blinking more rapidly.
And you were right.

Now you are a man
With a family of your own,
A house and responsibilities,
A long way from fireflies.
There are not nearly as many
Of them these summers
As there used to be.
Just like memories as I grow older.
But whenever I see
The blink of a firefly,
I think of you,
With love.

FOUNTAIN

A fountain fills a basin
Which overflowing
Fills a basin
Which overflowing
Fills a basin.

And so a parent
Fills a child with
Values, beliefs, and traditions,
Habits, morals, and directions.

What greater satisfaction
Than to see one's child
Implementing a parent's teachings,
Teaching those teachings to
His own child.

This is to know eternity,
A little piece of oneself
Left to continue
When life ends.

G.B.

If he were a Ninja Turtle,
He said,
He would be Botticelli,
Little Barrel.

I don't see him much now.
And then only in my dreams.
He tends to be in the background
When he is there at all,
And he never says anything.

During the final weeks
He would not let me see him.
Not even stand silently
In the corner of his darkened room.

I needed to tell him I loved him,
That I could not understand
How to live in a world
Without him.
But he was adamant.

I think of him now—

Whenever I hear a V
Of geese honking
Across the sky.

GRACE

Share your grace with me
That I might grow older
With dignity and class
As you do;

That I might awaken each morning
Eager to embrace
Being alive,
Working to make use of every moment
Given to me;

That I might love unconditionally
With all my heart
And welcome all people
Into my world;

That I might have the patience
To endure what I cannot change
And fight
For what is right;

That I might greet each moment with
A sense of humor
And a strong sense of self,
Taking life as it comes;

That I might know
That I have done my best
And live the rest of my life
Without regret.

HOUSE ARREST

I will hold you
With a
Fierce gentleness,
Softly tight,
Protecting you
From harm.
If I could put you in
An open cage,
I would.
How do I
Keep you safe,
And let you
Be free?

How

How do you thank someone
Who has saved your life,
More than once?

Who has waited for you,
In the dark?

Whom you could not push away,
No matter how hard you tried?

Who never gave up on you,
Despite the pain and struggle?

Who held you,
When you were scared?

Who loved you,
In spite of yourself?

How?

You cannot.

You can only appreciate
The person who has done this.

You can only cherish,
The person who has done this.

You can only marvel,
At your good fortune.

You can only wonder,
Why you deserve this treatment.

You can only hope,
That you are worthy.

You can only be,
With this miracle.

IF A TREE . . .

I need you to listen.
There is so much
I have to confess before you:
Guilt
Shame
Disappointment
Regret.
I have to seek
Your forgiveness
Before
It is too late.
You say that
There is no need,
Everything is fine.
You will not listen
To my pleas.
How different,
Our memories.
You remember everything as joyful,
Complete and loving,
But I have so many
Haunting visions of
My behavior
In the past.
Let me purge myself.
Let me release the awful pressure,
Or I will become like a tree,
Cracking,
Falling of its own weight
And weakness
To the forest floor—

Crashing down in pain,
Producing strong sound waves,
But making no noise.

INEXPRESSIBLE

You are not here tonight.
I am at the core of a swirling silence
Screaming to be heard.
Nothing to do but play
Solitaire on the computer
Or think.
Eventually I arrive at a place
Of piercing clarity
Where I realize that all the time
That could ever be
Would not be enough
To tell you all that I have to say.

Love is beyond verbal expression,
And each time I try
I fall short and hope there
Is enough time to try again,
To expand my words,
To get it right,
And then the fear that a time
Will come
When it is too late
And I am left with guilt, sadness,
A yearning
To be allowed to try once more.

I hope beyond hope
That despite my futile attempts
My lover will already know
What it is that I need
To say.

INVESTMENT

How time increases in value
As it slips away.
What was once forever,
Is now tomorrow.

Panic and pain strike
At thoughts of what was
Left undone, unsaid, unnoticed.

Gone forever.
Fostering regret and longing,
Sadness and melancholy.

Letting go is the hardest.
Now the investment is now:
Filling today completely.

No more wasted hours or minutes.
No more words left unsaid.
No more deeds left undone.

The past is gone.
Today is here.

IRONY

Life is irony.
When all is well
And secure,
It strikes.
The bottom falls out.
It is a trap
That's always set.
The expected consequence
Twists into
Surprise, pain, disappointment.
The shock
Deflates the world.
The grand plan,
Put together with
Care and love,
Becomes disaster.

January 20, 2017

Today there will be no news.
No TV or radio
No papers or magazines
No Ipad or laptop
No Iphone or computer.

I will spend the day in meditation,
Taking only water,
To purify myself
For the work to come.

My goals:
To make my mind a still lake
Reflecting my deepest beliefs.
To become balanced
And centered.

I will find my core,
The I
In the middle of the storm,
Peaceful and resolute
Despite the raging winds
All around it.

I will prepare myself
To take a stand,
To defend the basic ideal
That every being is the same,
Even those who oppose us,
All wanting happiness.
All deserving compassion.

All beings have the right
To an unencumbered life
Of dignity.

I am joining the army
Of the those who support
Life on Earth
In all its forms,
And in every way.

I will be a soldier,
Standing firm against
Hatred, prejudice,
Economic exploitation,
Pettiness, pollution,
The forces of poverty and disease,
Standing up for a world
Of interbeing,
Of peace,
Of respect,
Of freedom.

I am joining an army,
And this
Is my basic training.

Jigsaw

First find the straight edges
And form the frame;
The illusion of control,
Reigning in chaos,
The limits of the finite.

Each piece
With its crisp edges
Looking complete,
Meaningless on its own,
Real only when part of the whole
Where it ceases to exist.

Is there a line
Where the tree stops
And the sky begins?
A border between
The water
And the shore?
A point where
The rider stops and
The horse becomes?

We hold hands
Trading skin cells.
We breathe
Each other's breath.
And when our tongues touch,
We swallow each other.

Journey

We are like the hands of a clock:
Two unique entities
Each complete by itself;
Two unique entities
Each incomplete by itself.
Fully alive only when
Defining each other,
Together making meaning,
Counting down the
Hours and minutes of
Our short journey
In time.

Joy

I

Always yearning,
Never satisfied.
Lusting for something
Bigger, better
Newer, more advanced
Than what we
Already have.
Always hoping
That this time
We will be happy.
Waiting is not an option,
Which brings debt,
Which brings more
Discomfort, unease.
We are hungry ghosts,
Never sated,
Always missing today
While we look
To future acquisitions.
We are caught on
The hamster wheel
Of more.
Rushing nowhere,
Passing by
And leaving
The joy behind.

II

We do not have
To wait for joy.
It is everywhere,
Easy to find.
Think of
The new wife
Who makes
An Easter egg hunt
In a single room,
Small toys for prizes;
Or the mother
And her child
Making paper cones
Filled with flowers
To put at
Neighbors' doors
Early in the morning
On May first;
An infant raising its arms
To be lifted
From the crib.
Moments of joy
Are everywhere,
All around us.
Here.
Now.

JULY 16, 2020

I
Am the
Eye
Of the storm.
In my
Green bubble,
Chaos and disease
All around
Me,
The Solipsist.
Cracks
Will
Happen.
And then
What?

KENSHO

A dream came to me last night.
I was part of some subgroup
Of a large convention
In a hotel
Doing a project or
Preparing a presentation
With others.
At some point
I led a group of people
To the top of
Northfield Mountain
Looking for the truth.
When we reached the peak,
We found nothing.
All at once I understood
What Buddhists call emptiness.
Empty your mind
They say.
That does not mean
To think about nothing.
It means empty your mind.
And that is the answer.
The meaning of it all
Is that there is no meaning of it all.
When you strip away
All the layers,
There is nothing underneath.
Like trying
To find the substance
Beneath the attributes.

LESSON FROM KEATS

Life is change.
To stay the same is to die.

Consider the figures
On a Grecian urn.
Mad, glorious reveling
Without motion.
Lovers racing
With no movement.
Eternal,
Never changing
Activity
With no Action.
How wonderful
To be forever.
But the poet warns:

O Attic shape! Fair attitude! with brede
    Of marble men and maidens overwrought,
With forest branches and the trodden weed;
    Thou, silent form, dost tease us out of thought
As doth eternity: Cold Pastoral!

As cold as death itself,
This silent, static scene.
An endless now,
A single second frozen.
A trap,
No end to youth and love and celebration,
"Too happy" to be real.
Not of our living world.

Life is impermanence,
To be permanent is to die.

LINE

How thin the line
Between here and
Not here.
How arbitrary
The crossing,
Willful
Or not.
One misstep,
One wrong turn.
I am now just realizing
How close we came.
Like missing the lottery by one number
Or being acquitted by one vote.
What about next time?
Anywhere, any time, any way.
What would I do
Without you?
Where would us go?
Do we exist
As individuals
After so many
Years?
Or are we wed
More deeply
Than on our wedding day?
Wed in heart and mind and soul.
We have become conjoined,
Our fates bound together.
You or me,
It does not matter.
For now
We still are.

Love's Metrics

I love you as the ocean loves the shore,
The wind plays in the trees, the sunshine warms
The earth. Can these three pictures and no more
Explain my feelings when I'm in your arms?

They're not enough to tell my love for you.
I love you as the clouds float in the sky,
The stars shine through the night, the bachelors woo
The maids. Can these explain your gentle sigh?

I love you as the bird protects its nest,
The moms embrace their babes, the soldier holds
Her post. I lay my head upon your breast.
Is there no way to show that you are gold?

To measure love is not within my skills,
I only know that yours gives my heart thrills.

MARCH 13, 1971

Oh Daffodil, Daffodil,
We are still together,
Through beautiful days
And stormy weather.

Oh Daffodil, Daffodil.
On that night I bade you stay,
But you were scared
And ran away.

Oh Daffodil, Daffodil,
Then you returned.
It had to be because
For both our hearts the other yearned.

Oh Daffodil, Daffodil,
When I look back to that day,
I am amazed how long
Has been our way.

O Daffodil, Daffodil,
Then we had endless time to play,
But now we cannot lose a day,
Because we have turned old and gray.

MEDITATION

I take my seat
Before the icon,
The candle in between.
I follow my breath,
Belly rising
Belly falling.
All is silence.
My goal:
To quiet my mind
And open a path
For vipashyana
To work its miracles.
And by thinking of this,
I fail.
The flickering, floating candle
Reflects the
Disquiet
Of my mind.
I am not ready.
Higher levels of
consciousness
Are not available
To me.
Intention has value.
To intend
To relieve suffering
In another
And fail,
Is a noble thing.
So all is not lost.
But what to do,

When trying itself
Can lead
Only to defeat?

MIRACLE

The miracle of compost.
A process so magical
That only God could understand.
Trash becomes
Nutrient-rich earth
For nourishing vegetables, fruits,
Flowers, and berries.
Like spinning straw into gold.
Transubstantiating garbage
Into something life-giving.

We all have trash in our minds:
Anger, fear, resentment, cruelty,
Sadness, guilt, revenge, bitterness.

Could we compost this garbage
By looking at it deeply
And learning from it?
Could we turn it into
A nutrient-rich substance
In which to plant seeds of
Peace, loving kindness, patience,
Forgiveness, compassion?

Could it nurture bodhichitta?

Would it make a good medium
For planting the seeds of enlightenment,
Growing our inner lotus seed,
Helping it to bloom?

Can we become
Self-composting?

Mirror

Who is that?
With the baggy eyes
Drawn face and
Gray beard?

The picture in my head,
The one I see
When I am talking to someone,
Or remembering,
Or dreaming,
Is much younger.

Where did I go?
I don't remember
Leaving.
I've always been
Here.

Some kind of trick,
I assume
Because it can't be true.

MOTHER

A mother's path is paved in love and tears,
The kind that knows no bounds
Or limits,
Razor focused,
That lasts forever.
Sometimes she leads, guiding.
Sometimes she follows, learning.
Sometimes she walks beside, being a friend.
She'll never stop,
Committed for life.
A bond that cannot be broken.
A connection that cannot be cut.
This child was once
A physical part of her.
No less a part of her now.
Tethered with infinite length
And endless time.

MR. KITSEL

Where did you go, Mr. Kitsel?
With your tickling fingertips
That made me squeal with delight?
Years later
I needed your help
Making the crossing
From boy to man, Mr. Kitsel,
But you were gone.
I did not realize then that you
Had already shown me the way,
So I made many wrong turns
And traveled down dark roads,
Disappointing myself
And others,
Before understanding,
Now that I am older than you ever were,
What you had taught me:
Being a man
Did not mean being macho,
But being kind, loving unconditionally.
Men are generous and supportive.
They have a sense of humor.
Real men accept and support others.
They find the joy in life
And feel strongly,
Even if it means crying.
I wonder, Mr. Kitsel,
Can you see me now?
Can you hear me?
Do you forgive me my faults?
Are you proud of my good qualities?

Have I become the man
You showed me how to be?
If you can,
Mr. Kitsel,
Please give me your blessing
Today.

Mud

Om mani padma hum—

What good is mud?
Cars get stuck in it
People slip and fall in it
Whole houses are crushed by it.

The lotus seed grows in the mud
Below brackish waters.

The seed sends up a stalk
Which ultimately bursts
Into a precious gem,
A blossom so special
That it forms
The thrones
For Buddhas and Bodhisattvas.

Some say we are made from mud.
Under our skin we are
Slippery and wet and opaque.
Like mud.

And we are born
Containing a seed deep
In the mud of our minds.

If
We notice it
Nurture it
Water it
Feed it,

It too will
Send up a stalk
Ending in a magnificent
Blossom,
Our realized potential,
Wisdom,
The clear vision of reality.
Enlightenment.

This may take a whole lifetime,
Or thousands of lifetimes,
But we each contain this
Possibility
Of becoming
What we have the good fortune
To be able to become.

If we pay attention.

— Behold, the jewel in the lotus.

Need

Now that we are old,
You and I,
There is no time
To waste.

My heart fills my chest
And needs to open
To you
While there is time.

After so many years
Who would have thought
That there was so much more to say?
We thought we had forever.

Even forever might not be enough
To share such profound feelings
That they cannot be
Expressed in words.

Eyes to eyes
Heart to heart
Hand to hand
Breath to breath.

> "O, I have ta'en
> Too little care of this"
> *King Lear* (III, iv, 36-7)

My dark glasses,
The one with lenses
Made of ego,
Often blind me
To the story lines which cross my path.

My sweet bride wore a blusher
Just to please me.
I know she did this
Because she told me so
Several days later.

He took his first steps
Towards me in the hotel room.
I was declaiming on
My academic prowess
And barely caught the sight.

I was standing waist deep in the river
Engaged in conversation to my right.
You had to signal me from the shore
To look left
To see our flailing son.

A goldfish in a bowl
Swimming in endless circles
Stopping occasionally
To argue with
Its reflection.

Peach Trees

The dead winter branches
Push out leaves
And then the pink dress
Dripping pollen,
Inviting bees and others
To make love and fruit.
Gestation continues
Through late summer.
The air fills with sweetness,
The tree dropping
Gold and red offerings
Which will rot
In just a few days.
So fast, this life.
Then the tree
Drops its leaves,
Becomes dead winter branches,
Again.

PEACHES

Do the peaches know anything
After living an entire life
In less that a year,
Coming to fruition and death
All at once?
Who teaches them
What to do?
Do they put on knowledge
With their golds and reds,
Their sweet aroma
Lasting just a moment?
Do they understand
Any of this:
Why they are,
Where they came from
Where they are going?
The cycle goes on,
Automatically,
Without thought,
Without awareness.
The peaches know
Nothing.
They do
Nothing.
They just are.

PEEPERS

Nature's Greek chorus,
The peepers,
Have much to say.
They speak with urgency
In a language unknowable.

Are they warning me?
Are they voicing their approval?
Perhaps they're indifferent.
They could be laughing at me
Smugly from their position
Of secret knowledge.

Their song is
Full of meaning.
Isn't it?

PLATO'S CAVE

Even you,
With your immense spiritual
Strength,
Your limitless
Love,
Your infinite
Devotion,
And absolute
Dedication,
Could not lift me out
Of the dark hole
I had dug for myself.
You dropped ladders and ropes.
You built scaffolds.
I could not move,
As if held
By some force
I could not see.
I could find no motivation.
You sat by the edge
Waiting.
You would have waited forever.
In time
I struggled out.
As if emerging from Plato's cave,
I was blinded by the light of day.
No memory,
No understanding,
No energy.
Only you—
Holding out a hand.

Rainbow

She burst into the restaurant
Announcing
"There is a double rainbow."

People left what they were doing
To step outside
To take a look
Holding up
Their phone cameras

Magnificent,
An archway offering
Endless possibilities;
A miracle,
A sudden painting
In the sky,
So ephemeral,
Apparently
Out of nothing.

Of course
One could explain
The whole thing
With talk of visible light,
Refraction, and so on.

But that would be like
Reducing human emotion
To electro-chemical reactions
In the brain.

Where do those reactions come from,

Those emotions
Which bind us as humans,
Which give us a glimpse
Of the Universal,
Of power
We cannot understand?

There has to be more
To rainbows
And humanity
Than physics and chemistry.

A person should
Never miss
An opportunity
To see a rainbow.

RESISTANCE

The Icon is still.
The beads are still.
The air is still.
No sounds.
The only movement
Is the hopping flame,
Reflecting the undisciplined mind.
Concentrating on the breath,
Settling into the rhythmic
In and out,
Does not bring ease and insight.
The self resists desperately.

RESPONSIBILITY

Who am I?
And why am I
Who I am?

Am I responsible for
My behavior?
Or am I like Oedipus,
Destined at birth
To fulfill my destiny,
Regardless of what I do
Or the choices I make?

Have I been constructed by
My parents,
My mother's distrust
And paranoia,
My father's depression
And kindness?

Have I been shaped by
My experiences,
Triumphs and failures,
Learning to fear
Disappointment and thus
Always playing it safe?

Am I the product
Of forces beyond my control,
Like genetics?
Then how can I be responsible?
I have made some terrible choices,
Hurting others and myself.

I always knew
The right thing to do.
I knew how to act with kindness
And love and respect,
But my shining horses of
Good intention so often
Were held back by a dark force
Who held the reins.

So who am I?
Am I the one responsible
For all the pain
And disappointment
My actions gave to others?

Or am I a piece on
A giant chess board,
Moved by an invisible hand?

Is the answer crucial,
Or simply irrelevant?

Ride

Windows up
Radio off
Ninety miles to go

My mind turns like
A water mill
Making me-grist
Which forms thoughts
Which fill the space

Is there any value?
Can I make something lasting?
Is there anything next?
Is it all just
Birth, old age, sickness, and death?

Am I floating or
Standing on the ground?

Do I have a purpose?
Where am I going?

The car stops
I open the door
And step into life.

Risk

The risk of relationships.
Real relationships
Of deep connection
And interweaving,
Hard work
Acceptance
Support
Selflessness,
Where you endure
The unendurable,
Allow
The unallowable,
Embrace
The unembraceable.

So much investment
For something that
Will inevitably
End,
If nothing else, in death,
Leaving you bereft.

We could avoid the risk,
Not become involved with another,
Keep everything
On the surface.
The shallowness is all.

But we take the risk
Despite the pain
We know is coming

To know for
Even one second
We are not
Alone.

SPIRIT

A new teacher
A new job
A new school
A new town
A new state.

We explored the
Fields and brooks and woods
Of our latest home.
Never before
Had we been in such
A rural spectacle.

Wandering through the woods
I looked up.
There you were,
Naked,
In all your soft beauty,
Open to it all.

I wish I had had
Your spirit.

Storm

Like an invading army
The storm assaults the outer walls,
Lashing them with wind and rain.
Howling gusts,
Flailing trees.
Our little house will stand
Because it has to.
That is its purpose.
Even if the lights go out
And the water won't run
We will be OK.
The wood stove at its heart
Will warm us enough
To get through this night.
We have won
Against stronger storms
That have rattled our lives and love.
We had to.
That was our purpose.
Our single heart gave off
Enough heat to keep us alive.
We had given our word,
We swore an oath.
We did.
We swore an oath

SURVIVAL

The mind is designed
For survival.

The brain takes unfortunate events,
Sad, angry, shameful,
Processes and
Integrates them,
Filing them safely away,
And moves on.

But what if a stain
Or a scar remains—
A continuous reminder
Of that which
We most want to forget?

The strength of the memory
Is the strength of the original.
The spontaneous overflow
Of powerful emotions
Recollected in turmoil.

The brain broils
In its own heat.
The memory will not
Cede space,
Will not yield to more pleasant memories.

Festering,
Punishing,
Dominating
The imagination.

There is no moving on.
Only being stuck
In an endless cycle,
No way to get off.

Drowning in a maelstrom—
No one to help
To throw a rope
To pull one out.

THANKSGIVING

Thanksgiving.
We go around the table,
Each expressing thanks
For someone or something
Of personal importance.
The years have come and gone.
Now I am the oldest,
Which means that I go first.
I feel pressure
To say something wise and profound,
But oldest or not,
I am still just me.

Six months ago,
My soul-mate
Stood on the edge
Of the Abyss,
Looked in,
And stepped back.
I realized then that
The line between being and not being
Is razor thin.

We cannot wait until Thanksgiving,
Once a year,
To declare aloud that
We are thankful for each other,
That we love each other,
That we cherish each over.
We must say these things aloud
Every day, while we can.

That was the wisdom
I imparted
This Thanksgiving.

THE OLD KNIGHT

Rocinante—,
Over here.
I have a question.
Where is your rider,
The old knight?
There are windmills
 Sprouting everywhere.
Their blades
Are chopping up society,
The whole world.
Everything
Is falling apart.
We need someone
Like him
Right now.
Someone with real ideals,
With conviction,
Without fear.
There is so little time,
And I hate to bother him
In his retirement,
But without
A hero,
We are lost.

THE POET IMAGINES HIS FINAL CONVERSATIONS

An avalanche of white has pinned me down.
I'm peeing through a tube into a bag.
No dignity is left one at the end,
As life slips by and there's no turning back.

First comes my loving bride, my life-long friend
And prop, supporting me until the end.
Her smile fixed protecting me from pain.
Again she does not want to worry me.

There's so much left to say between us both.
Forgiveness to be sought and offered forth.
A love that we cannot express in words.
We make no sound but sit in silence now.
Our hearts already know all that's to know.

She holds my hand and looks into my eyes.
No braver soul than hers I've ever seen.
If only she would once more say to me
That I'm her hero as I was before,
Regardless if she lies or tells the truth.
Then peace and satisfaction would be mine.

To look on death is not so bad it seems,
But bidding love farewell takes all my strength.
She then withdraws so others may approach.
Then comes my son, my greatest work of art.

His face all wrinkled, trying not to cry,
So sensitive to loss and others' pain

He cannot speak nor can he look away.
So I must speak for both of us myself
And bring back memories of fishing trips
And baseball games and Halloween parades,
Of soccer games and birthday festivals,
Of fatherhood, both his and mine as well.

He slowly backs away. He wants to stay,
And yet he goes. There's not much he can do.
And in his place my brother looks at me.
The only sibling whom I've ever had.

We've grown apart, who once were closely knit.
A birthday call each year and not much more.
But if and when I need him, he is there
To be my help, and that alone demands
My love. He tries to see the world in terms
Of practicality. Our deaths will come.
Acceptance is the only thing to do.
But confrontation this direct is hard
For him to face, and practicality
Gives way to grief, regret, and loss.
Too much to bear. He looks into my eyes
To say good-bye and turns to hide his grief.

What have we here? The children of my son,
So young, confused, and scared of this strange sight.
What do they know of death, infinity,
The absolute? Their Papa is about
To leave forever for some other world.
Their reticence says all they know to say.

I sing their praises and my love for them,
Predicting greatness for their future lives
And tell them of my pride in all they are.

I ask that they should think of me from time
To time, and when they see a star at night.
I will be with them in all future times.
So don't be sad. Remember me with joy.

And last my daughter, wife to my only son,
A woman of great strength, so resolute,
But now gone soft with sadness and with love.
The sorrow will not last, but hopefully
The love goes on while I prepare to go.

Now all is quiet, peaceful and at ease.
The tension gone, the final moment's here.
I see them all and fill with joy because
They're here, with me, to see me off today
So I can leave in peace and gratitude,
To what will come, to learn the secret next.

The Sweet Sorrow Of Parting

You always had to leave.
I would rush from place to place,
Looking through the trees,
Looking between the buildings,
Looking from the hill,
Until your car was gone.

I floated to my room
Like a man under water,
Oppressed by a smothering silence,
Numb inside and out,
Disconnected, unmoored, unhappy.

The little room seemed so big.
The toothbrush was no longer giggling.
The desk chair had stopped singing.
The narrow bed was much too wide.

Clutching my only hope.
You would come back again.
You would come back.
I knew you would come back.

I know you will come back.

THE TRUTH?

As elusive as a dream
Floating away
As we awaken.
We sort of remember
And fill in the rest.

Memory contains
An element of imagination,
Contaminants
Impurities.

The absolute truth we seek
Is not in this world
Where everything is fiction.

The Unknown Season

Dragging ourselves
Out from under winter,
We reset the clocks.
There is new light,
More light,
Longer light,
Offering hope of renewal,
Of rebirth.
But the cycle of the seasons
Is a metaphor,
Not a duplicate,
Of our lives.
The flecks of snow
In my beard
Do not melt away.
They proliferate
As the wrinkles deepen.
Only one cycle,
Where winter leads
To an unknown
Which is not called
Spring.

"There's A Special Providence in The Fall of a Sparrow"

Who will mourn for the dead bird
Lying stiffly on the path,
Sightless,
Flightless,
Lifeless?

Where is the funeral procession
Of birds flying in a row
Slowly overhead?
Are there only ants?

Why is there no master bird
Standing over the dead,
Wings spread
Invoking eternity?

At least Nature should take note
Of the loss of one of its own.
There is no thunder, no rain,
No lightening, no
Shaking earth.

Surely "There's a special providence
In the fall of a sparrow."

TRUE LOVE

Does true love exist?
The love
Of romance novels,
Of the movies,
Of our dreams?

A love of sacrifice
That always puts the other first,
That is always supportive,
That is always present,
That is always devoted?

A love eternal
That knows no bounds,
That never falters,
That is absolute,
That is always pure?

A love so consuming
That the self dissolves
Into a fine mist
Inhaled by the other
Where it rests

Protected
On waves of
Liquid warmth,
One with the other,
One breath,

One movement
In tandem,
One.

This love does exist.
I know.
I know because
I have been loved this way.

Turning Back The Clocks

We have turned back the clocks
And the darkness oppresses me,
Like living in a box, a coffin
With only dim light and a suffocating
Sense of palpable silence
Echoing in my ears.
I have not felt this alone
Since the distant past.
It is as if someone has died
And the world has gone dormant
In mourning.
When will the shadow lift?
When will I sing again?
When will this weight lift
From my heart?
There is no end
That I can see.
My future is getting shorter.
Is this the way it will end?

Uncertainty

The goddess,
Guide and guardian,
Has led me to
The gates of Hell.
The heat.
The pain.
Why am I here?
I don't know what to do.
I don't know how to act.
I don't know what to say.
I don't know where to go.

I thought I understood
The world.
But now everything is confused:
Up and down—
In and out—
Top and bottom—
Right and wrong.

I want to go back
To the place I was in
Yesterday.
A place that made sense,
If there still is,
Or ever was
Such a place.

How do I get there?
Which is the way to go?

Who can tell me?

Because

I don't know what to do.

UNIVERSE

The universe doesn't care.
In fact,
It doesn't do anything.
It is.
Take star production, for instance.
Does the universe plan this,
Choosing a particular time and place and method?
Does it worry about making too few
Or too many stars?
Does it care if a nearby planet
Is destroyed in the process?
Does it find making stars
To be gratifying?
Nope.
Astrogenesis is a process
Bounded by the laws of physics
Which are part of
What the universe is.

The universe reminds one
Of the Old Testament law:
Absolute
Right or wrong
Obeyed or not obeyed
An eye for an eye
Punishment swift and harsh.
The law does not play favorites
Or apply to one and not another.
If you break it,
You pay.
The law does not care.
The law just is.

But then there was Jesus.
He brought mercy to the law.
Suddenly there were
Extenuating circumstances,
Context,
Forgiveness,
Even second chances.
Jesus brought humaneness
To the law.

In a way
We do this too,
To the universe.
We cannot prevent the volcano
From destroying the city
Or the tsunami from
Drowning hundreds of thousands.
But we can mourn for the dead.
We can help rebuild.
We can care and be kind
And forgive and love.
And since we're a part of the universe,
We bring these characteristics to it.

We're so small,
But we have volition.
We can plan.
We can enjoy or mourn.

We can bring all this
To the universe.
And that is what makes us
Extraordinary.

Us

Like sperm and egg
We came together
To create a new life,
Part of each and unique,
Individual and combined.
New growing pains,
A new adolescence,
Maturing again,
Tears and smiles,
Triumphs and defeats,
And always hope.
We are two branches
From the new tree we made,
Together and apart,
Separately we grow as one,
The same sap
Flowing in both.
We are not who we were,
And we are.

VOICE

Discovered—
On the backs
Of envelopes
And under the rug,
Your voice
Speaking powerfully
Your pleasure and pain
For all the world,
To influence others,
To be counted,
To be known,
To become
A force.
Are there
Other voices,
Under the
Sofa cushions,
Behind
The desk drawers?
Waiting quietly,
Balling up
In the bottoms of pockets,
Turning to shreds
Behind the dryer.

Voices rejected
By the profits
Of publication,
The fashions
Of the times.
Now,
When the need
For poetry is great,
So many voices
Sing into
The void.

"We are such stuff
As dreams are made on; and our little life
Is rounded with a sleep."
(*The Tempest*, Act 4, scene 1, 156–158)

Searching for reality, the truth,
Examining the fabric of existence,
I find only fabrication.

Bits of perception,
Like black flies,
Invade us continually.

Sights and textures
Smells and sounds
Colors and shapes
The tastes of life

Combine in the ovens
Of our brains,
Baked into the cake of reality.
We improvise:
More sugar
A little chocolate,
Decorations.

And each of us
Calls the cake true.
Just ask to eye-witnesses—
Two different stories.

We invent along the way
As yesterday fades from view
And the present unfolds
Into the future.

WHAT WOULD JESUS DO?

The sin was great
But she was ill
Was stuck in bed
Could not arise

She called the church
Asked for a priest
Who said he could
Not hear her words
Unless she came
Herself to church
And left to go
About his work

Would God do this?
Give precedence
To form alone
To first the rite
Before the need
Before the care?

Mercy was what
Jesus had taught
Love all beings
To help and heal
To help bring peace

The priest was wrong
Ignoring pain
Ignoring need
Because the form
Had to be right

Before he'd act
And thus the end

He missed the chance
To do his work
To bring her peace
To soothe her soul
To lift the burden
Holding her down

She was alone
Adrift at sea
Nowhere to turn
But to look up
She would confess
To god himself
And he would hear
He would forgive
Because her words
Were strong and true
He would accept
And heal her needs
Despite the priest
Who could not see
The truth, that he
Had more urgent
Work than seeing
That rites were done
Before he sought
To heal the soul
That called to him
In hour of need.

WINDOWS

The new windows are in,
The glass so clean
That it disappears.
It makes no impositions,
Puts no conditions
On the view.
Already
Dust begins to coat the panes.
There will be smears.
There will be rain drops.
There will be fingerprints.
There will be bird shit.
The view will be obscured.
People will clean the windows,
Trying to bring them back
To their original condition.
But there will be dirt left
In the corners.
There will be streaks.
The original clarity
Likely will never come back.

Zeus Moment

I would like a Zeus moment
When someone splits open
My head,
Not to birth
A goddess,
But to release my anger,
Letting it fly away
To wherever anger goes,
Leaving a space
Where it had been,
An empty drawer
I could fill
With calm, kindness, and compassion.

ACKNOWLEDGEMENTS

§

ONCE AGAIN I want to thank Dede Cummings for making this project possible. Thanks to Nancy Olson for her generously agreeing to read and comment on the manuscript. I always appreciate the love and support of my family, Ben, Pam, Anthony, and Namiah. Most of all, I need to acknowledge the love of my life, without whom nothing happens, Nina. And of course, I cannot forget my constant companion, Socrates.

Daniel A. Heller was a secondary educator for over thirty years. He holds a BA and an MA in English from Middlebury College, an MEd from Keene State College (NH), a CAGS in educational administration and planning from UVM, and an honorary Doctor of Humanities degree from The College of St. Joseph (Rutland, VT). He has published six books on education. This is his second book of poetry, although he has written poetry since he was in his teens. He lives in Brattleboro, Vermont, and Hartford, Connecticut, with his wife of over forty-five years, Nina.

§